Old PEEBLES

by

Rhona Wilson

The Tweed is the fourth longest river in Scotland, behind the Tay, the Spey and the Clyde. Although it is the only true border river, it s
from England for just a twelve mile stretch between Coldstream and Paxton. The river's source is at Tweed's Well near the Peebless
border, only a few miles from that of the Clyde which runs parallel for about the first twelve miles of its course. The rivers' proximit
one time prompted schemes to create a confluence between them. If Clyde waters were diverted into the shallower Tweed, it was suggested, this
would increase the river's navigable length. Due to alternative transport developments, nothing came of the idea and so the Tweed, with its awkward
gravel banks, has remained largely traffic-free.

Jenny Dalgleish
Chief Maid of Honour

Mary Paterson

Abigail Mason

Nellie Dickman
Beltane Queen

Mary Brydon

PEEBLES
BELTANE QUEEN
AND
MAIDS OF HONOUR
22ND JUNE 1906

Lizzie Porteous

Florence Whyte

© Stenlake Publishing, 1998
First published in the United Kingdom, 1998,
by Stenlake Publishing
Telephone / Fax: 01290 551122

ISBN 1 84033 044 9

The Beltane Festival originates from an ancient Celtic festival celebrating 'Baal's fire', the power which brought light, warmth and growth in the early summer. In Peebles this festival evolved into two separate events, a sporting celebration and a Christian event, both of which were attended by important figures of the day such as King James IV. The day-long festival had a revival in the 1890s when it was decided to resume the Riding of the Marches (a check of the town's boundary stones). To involve the town's youth, the first Beltane Queen was crowned in 1899 with thousands gathering to witness the ceremony on the steps of the Old Parish Church. The Beltane celebrations are still held and have been extended to cover a full week.

INTRODUCTION

Peebles appears as 'Peblis' in old records, its origin attributed by Rev. William Dalgleish in the late eighteenth century to the pebbles in its soil. This straightforward explanation was much mocked by later historians; in 1834 Rev. John Elliot opined that it was derived from the Celtic word 'Pebyll' meaning 'moveable dwelling or temporary encampments'. Peebles gained royal favour at an early stage in its history for several reasons. Alexander III, who built its Cross Kirk in 1260, favoured the town as a summer residence on account of its hunting grounds and David II made it a Royal Burgh in 1367. The change in status was probably a reward for the loyalty of its inhabitants as ten years earlier the town had helped free the king from imprisonment by the English by helping to pay their ransom demand of 100,000 merks.

Although Peebles is considered peaceful for a border town – 'as quiet as the grave – or Peebles' as Lord Cockburn once quipped – it has had its share of troubles in the past. In 1545 it was almost completely burned down by the Earl of Hertford who left little standing apart from the churches. A similar fate was suffered, this time by accident, around 1604 and in the mid-seventeenth century the town had to endure occupation by Cromwell and his army as he attempted to capture Neidpath Castle. Invasions and attacks such as these influenced the building of the new town which subsequently sprung up on the east side of the Tweed because this area was easier to defend. A substantial town wall (a part of which still stands on Venlaw Road) and gates existed until the Union of 1707.

By the 1790s Peebles was considered wealthy. It was said that the town and surroundings were of more 'an Italian than a Scottish landscape' and it attracted rich proprietors throughout that century on account of this beauty and its proximity to the cities of Edinburgh and Glasgow. During this period local industry and agriculture prospered. From 1728 to 1840 the Board of Manufacture appointed and paid skilled individuals to sort, staple and wash tarred wool in the town, a policy which improved the indigenous sheep farming industry and which benefitted the handloom weavers and tweed mills in turn. Improvements in other areas, however, were not always looked upon as being positive. Enclosure of farms, for example, meant that many of the smaller cottagers were chased off the land and the First Statistical Account of 1792 claimed that the population had decreased by over 25% as a result of this practice over the course of the previous century.

During the nineteenth century, Peebles escaped traditional industrial development as it had neither coal, sandstone nor workable limestone. Its position on a slow moving river also meant that water power could not be relied upon to fuel the mills established by the Thorburns and the Ballantynes in the late 1800s (although by the 1950s both companies were generating their own electricity to overcome this problem). Nevertheless, the town developed with a flurry of activity around the 1830s. Around fifty houses (some enlarged specifically for the town's weavers) went up at the start of the decade with the town council providing flour, barley and corn mills at the same time. The population doubled from just over 2,000 in 1801 to 4,059 in 1881. Most of this growth occurred from 1850 and is attributable to incomers arriving to work in the tweed mills and the growth of local tourism. The railways, which were established by the mid-1860s, were of great benefit to both trade and visitors and so also contributed to the population growth.

Today, Peebles main industry is that cemented by the establishment of the Peebles Hydropathic in the 1880s. This hotel has been joined by over twenty others to cater for its successful tourism industry and the well-stocked, specialist shops are evidence of the money that continues to come into the town. In the end its calm and pretty visage has been its fortune, with the Scottish Borders Council obviously investing a great deal of money – and rightly so – to keep it that way.

Peeblesshire's Coat of Arms show three parallel salmon: the centre fish swimming upstream, the other two swimming downstream. They symbolise the town's ancient motto, 'Contra Nando Incrementum', meaning 'there is increase by swimming against the stream'. This rather independent slogan refers to the salmon's annual ascension up the Tweed to reproduce.

This *c*.1908 photograph shows a cauld in the foreground which can be used by salmon to navigate the river. The Tweed's gentle flow has proved useless as a source of industrial power, its pools and shallows being a more friendly environment for salmon and trout. Its gravely bottom and lack of overhanging woods make it a particularly good spawning and feeding ground. In the late nineteenth century, however, its resources were depleted by poaching, over-fishing and the district's new drainage system. Luckily, the Angling Improvement Association was formed to control local fishing and annually restock the river with young trout so that by the 1950s the Tweed was considered one of the best sporting rivers in Scotland.

PEEBLES.

The building with white gables in the background left was one of the Thorburn mills which were demolished in the 1960s. Tweed cloth, once Peebles' main export, was originally called 'twill' (pronounced as 'tweel'). It is supposed to have been corrupted to the modern name thanks to the bad handwriting of an English buyer in the mid-1820s. The industry really took off in the late nineteenth century with the establishment in 1875 of the Thorburn's Damdale and Tweedside Mills and the Ballantyne's March Street Mill ten years later. By the 1950s together they employed almost 1,000 people, mostly women, who processed the raw materials to the finished article. Due to the town's housing shortage, Damdale had to open a hostel at a house called 'The Mount' for some of its workers who travelled from as far as Castle Douglas and Kirkcaldy.

Peebles. On the Silvery Tweed.

In the early days of the mills, employees worked a twelve hour day weekdays (with a break of an hour and a half) and a half day on a Saturday. By the 1950s this regime was much improved as the average working week was just forty-four hours (with weekends off) and wages were paid 'according to a scientific basis and fixed according to the skill and class of the work of the employee.' The female employees, however, were paid a minimum wage of around three pounds less than the men which was hardly fair. Despite this, wage levels set by the Board of Trade regulations were considered generous and labour relations better than average. The buildings were kept in good condition and the management of both companies organised many social and sporting occasions with both March Street and Damdale going as far as setting up takeaway canteens for their workers.

Taken from the end of Tweed Bridge, this picture looks up Springhill Road. The bridge was either built or reconstructed in the fifteenth century and originally made of wood that was clad in stone. In response to complaints about its narrow girth it was widened, first by public subscription in 1834, and then by the Town Council in 1900. The only record of Peebles' magistrates ever passing the death sentence involves the bridge and dates back to 1623. Thomas Paterson, a weaver who lived in the Old Town, was accused of stealing six cows and a sheep at Acrefield; he only admitted stealing four sheep and was immediately sentenced to death by drowning. Bound with cords, he was held under the water at the bridge which provided a viewing gallery for the crowds above. Afterwards, the officers who drowned him were taken to a nearby alehouse for their dinner.

Chambers' *History of Peeblesshire* puts forward the somewhat unlikely suggestion that the name Horsburgh derives from an ancient settler named 'Horse' or 'Orse'. What is known, however, is that this castle belonged to the Horsburgh family until 1622 when they sold it to pay their debts. Structures such as this were known as peel towers, a term used mainly in the borders. Usually designed for defence, they were built of stone and lime and had three storeys. The ground floor was used to pen cattle, sheep and the surrounding inhabitants in times of danger, the second was a living area and the third was taken up by the bed chambers. During the fourteenth century, architecture developed to deal with more sophisticated methods of warfare and walls became much thicker with towers often being expanded into castles. It wasn't until the seventeenth century, when times were reasonably peaceable, that mansion houses' design evolved and features that once had a functional, protective use became decorative. Turrets, for example, became chambers and battlements became balconies.

Peebles Hydropathic was built on the southern slopes of Venlaw as upmarket accommodation for the town's increasing number of visitors. Its attractions included the bath and curative department which offered treatments previously only obtainable abroad. It also supplied Turkish, Russian, German, pine, ozone, brine and even electric light baths and guests could also sit up to their chins in mud imported from Italy. Rheumatism, gout and 'nerves' could be treated with the 'sun and air bath' (of German origin) which, seemingly designed for the brave only, was situated on the nearby hill top.

Disaster struck in 1905 when the Hydro was destroyed by fire. The alarm was raised one evening at eight o'clock and within just six hours all that was left was the lacy facade of the building. Around 100 guests were sitting at dinner when a smell of burning pervaded the dining hall, guessed by most to be a chimney on fire. It had originated near to the roof and when the seriousness of the situation was assessed it was decided to save as much from the lower floors as possible. Once the building was evacuated, locals helped staff to remove items such as paintings and the guests' valuables and laid them on the grass outside. Unfortunately this was too tempting for some and a degree of plundering occurred. The *Peeblesshire Advertiser* reported that in one case a bible and shaving brush were the only objects left of one guest's luggage – 'were the thieves afraid of The Book?' the paper asked.

The Hydropathic's own fire hose was positioned at the front of the hotel while the local Fire Brigade fought the flames from the rear. But it was a losing battle and as early as 8.40 p.m. the turrets at the west side had crashed. By 9.30 p.m. a further two were down and an hour later floors were falling in and windows melting. This rapid spread was attributed to the Hydro's woodwork, 'a rich pitch pine', but Peebles' lack of adequate fire-fighting facilities didn't help matters. At one point it was decided to send for the Edinburgh Fire Brigade but it would have taken the outfit two and a half hours using relays of horses to reach the town. Attempts to arrange a special train service to get more help also failed as the station had closed for the night by the time someone tried to contact it.

In the end the fire won, providing a spectacle which could be seen for miles around. 'This is all that's left of our lovely Hydro', lamented the sender of this postcard. Insurance only partly covered the damage but a replacement built by James Miller (the designer of the Glasgow Exhibition in 1901) was opened in 1907. During both World Wars the Hydro was requisitioned as a military hospital, but by the 1950s it had returned to its original purpose of lavishing luxury on its guests. With 200 rooms it is the largest hotel in the east of Scotland and still averages 20,000 guests a year. Some of its most famous have included the Rolling Stones who stayed in the early 1980s and were booked in as a Japanese group to preserve their anonymity. True to form, they had breakfast at 3 p.m., dinner at 3 a.m. and refused to let the then manager, Pieter Van Dijk, into their wing of the hotel.

The shop with the dormer window on the left of this view of Northgate was once a grain merchants. Next to it is the Masonic Hall; Peebles has had a lodge since 1716. To the right the most noticeable difference today is that the buildings have been realigned so that the Cross Keys Inn no longer stands apart from the rest.

The shaft of Peebles' Mercat Cross dates back to the fifteenth century and its sundial to the seventeenth. Originally sited at the head of the Old Town, the cross was moved to a spot near the junction of High Street, Eastgate and Northgate and has been through the wars. Despite its antiquity, it was neglected by Peebles Town Council who eventually ordered its removal in 1807. Sir Adam Hay stepped in and preserved the shaft and sundial at his King's Meadows residence until 1859 when the council decided to accept it back. After renovation the cross was given a new home in the quadrangle of the Chambers Institute where it stayed for forty years until it was moved back to its old site in the High Street. Today, the cross has been moved further back from where it stands in this picture to create more space for traffic. Its pedestal is much less imposing and functions also as a traffic island.

This picture of Northgate looks past the turret of Veitches' outfitters which still has its old fashioned shop fittings and, like many Peebles' shops, sticks to old customs such as half day closing on a Wednesday. Other old family retailers in town include McGrath's outfitters, Forsyth's butchers, Whitie's newsagent, Scott Brothers' ironmongers and the Castle Warehouse drapery.

Northgate, Peebles

A later picture of Northgate showing on the right the bar which was formerly the Central Hotel. In the past, Peebles had its own breweries; William Ker of Kerfield set one up in the late eighteenth century while the Potts family's brewery had premises in St Michael's Wynd in 1867. That year Potts would have had the opportunity to supply seven inns including the Crown (in High Street) and the Tweedbridge (the original building was later demolished in 1899 to allow for the widening of the bridge).

The Tontine Hotel was built in 1808 on the Tontine principle, a system of investment invented in France by Lorenzo Tonti in the 1650s. The amount of capital needed to finance a building was divided into shares of equal value and these could be bought in the name of anyone of any age with the agreement that 'the longest liver [had] the right to the whole'; Sir Duncan Hay of Houston, who was nominated when a baby, became the eventual inheritor of the Peebles hotel. The Tontine attracted a different type of customer from the Cross Keys Inn (Peebles' main hotel) on account of its fashionable ballroom. Bought by Trust Houses in 1922, it is now extended to adjoin the building on the right. It is the only building in High Street still to have its courtyard complete with the original cobblestones.

The Cross Keys Inn, formerly known as the Yett, was the main hotel in Peebles until the Tontine was built. It's not known exactly how old it is although the date 1653 is carved into one of its stones. The building wasn't used as a hotel until the early 1700s and was formerly the town house of the Williamson family; the initials 'WW' can be made out on the roof although the slates which form them aren't necessarily the originals. In 1769 Bishop Forbes of Leith wrote that it had been run by Vintner Ritchie in the past and he was later succeeded by his two daughters, one of whom, Marion, was supposedly the inspiration for the character of Meg Dodds in Walter Scott's novel *St Ronan's Well*. Inspiration for the well was taken from the chalybeate spring at nearby Innerleithen which became a fashionable resort in the early 1800s.

Marion Ritchie's independence and eccentricity was of great repute. She wasn't impressed by what she saw as the pretentiousness of the Tontine Hotel, nor by some of her own customers – she was famous for telling customers to 'gang hame to your wife and bairns' if she thought they'd had too much to drink. The current owners, who have managed the hotel and bar for just two years, claim that Marion's ghost still haunts the building.

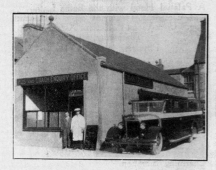
In the 1930s there was still very little car ownership in Peebles; this ad shows the alternative in the form of cars for hire. Wallace's Garage, close to the Railway Station, was well situated for tourists. (Altogether there were five other garages in Peebles at this time offering repair needs and services in addition to selling and hiring motors.) Bus companies, however, advertised themselves as the most comfortable form of transport for those wanting to tour the countryside around Peebles. For example, local businessmen Andrew Harper ran charabanc coach tours throughout the 1920s and early '30s, offering day trips to Moffat, Abbotsford, Manor (including Black Dwarf's Cottage), and Cademuir. Harper was successful enough to own 27 buses by the time he sold the business to the Caledonian Omnibus Company in 1932.

Apart from the usual businesses such as bakers and butchers, Peebles' High Street also has many small and flourishing specialist shops. Although these seemed to be in decline in the early 1960s when several old family businesses closed or changed hands, the smaller outlets have come into their own again and have been helped greatly by the tourist industry.

Peebles' North British Railway Station, pictured probably before 1914. At the start of the 1800s Peebles' main public transport was the stagecoach to and from Edinburgh. This was William Wilson's 'Caravan', drawn by a single horse which took ten hours to complete the twenty-two mile journey. By 1806 a new service, 'The Fly', used two horses to half the journey-time, although the infrequency of its service meant that it transported a maximum of only twelve passengers a week. Mr Croall's stagecoaches had shortened the journey to a three hour stretch by 1825, but this still couldn't satisfy some of the Edinburgh businessmen who were beginning to settle in the town and were clamouring for a railway.

Initial attempts to get a railway to Peebles failed because there wasn't the industrial and commercial urgency present in other towns which needed transport to develop their coal, iron and steel industries. It wasn't until the necessary Act of Parliament was passed in 1853 that the railway became a reality in Peebles and the line opened a couple of years later. In 1861 the line was leased in perpetuity by the Peebles Railway Company to the North British Railway. Three years later the NBR financed an extension to Innerleithen and Galashiels with the Caledonian Railway later opening up a western line to Symington and Glasgow. Despite a concerted effort by Liberal MP David Steel in the late 1960s, Peebles railway was closed and is now the site of the Edinburgh Road (its former course recognisable by the grass embankments). A small brown and cream hut (now business premises) near Somerfield Supermarket is the only part of the station which remains.

A favourite dare for local boys was to run through the long tunnel which leads on to the viaduct while trains were running. Nearby is Neidpath Castle, one of the best preserved of the district's ancient peel towers. These simple structures were an important communal defence against raids on horses, cattle and sheep. Built just a few miles apart, on alternate sides of the Tweed, each took part in an early warning system; at the first sign of trouble the nearest tower would light a fire on its roof which would be seen by its neighbour who would in turn light its own fire and so on. In this way the news could travel the seventy miles from Berwick to Bield in just a few hours. Despite Neidpath's antiquity (it was probably originally built in the twelfth century) it has few stories of battles and attacks attached to it. One of the few incidents in its history which prompted outrage was when the Duke of Queensberry felled its woodlands. Even years later, Wordsworth was moved to label him, 'Degenerate Douglas/Oh the unworthy Lord'.

An A.E.C. bus, owned by Andrew Harper of Peebles, at the Hydro. Although Harper's bus services were taken over by the Caledonian Omnibus Company, they themselves gave control of these to Western S.M.T. the following year.

The Green Tree Hotel's namesake flourished until the late 1950s when it was cut down to make way for the new reception and toilet block. The original part of the building (now the bar) probably dates back to the late nineteenth century. Venlaw Road, running down the left of this picture to what was at one time the railway marshalling yard, was once the local lovers' lane.

Between 1801 and 1803 the explorer Mungo Park was a doctor in Peebles, running his surgery from this dilapidated building in Main Street. Born in 1771, he was only 24 when he was chosen by the Africa Association to lead an expedition to source the Niger. With just six African companions he set out into unmapped territories and suffered terrible hardships, being kidnapped at one point by Arab tribesmen. His return to Britain after eighteen months was noticeable for its lack of ceremony; a few nights after his arrival on a slave boat, his family in Selkirk were woken by a knocking at the door. 'That'll be our Mungo,' offered a brother, 'I did see him get out of the coach in the square today.' He married and settled down in Peebles but couldn't resist the opportunity to complete the Niger mission when he was invited to head a government expedition in 1804. This time his party of forty were particularly unlucky. Only eleven men, including Park, reached the Niger alive and while travelling on the river they themselves perished when their boat either struck a rock or was ambushed by natives.

Forrester's Temperance Hotel (now the Keg) was built on the site of Park's surgery. The roots of Scotland's temperance movement lie in the cultural acceptance of alcohol in the early nineteenth century. In 1822 the government cut the duty on spirits by over two thirds which more than doubled consumption towards the end of the decade. In reaction to this, Temperance Societies began to appear throughout Scotland and although their initial pleas were merely for moderation in consumption, to 'improve conditions in the slums' for example, this quickly developed into demands for total abstinence, a movement given impetus in 1846 by the passing of a prohibition law in Maine, USA. By the 1890s 'dry' hotels such as Forrester's began to appear, although on the east coast establishments run on Gothenburg principles were very popular. These were pubs whose aim was to promote moderate alcohol consumption with all profits ploughed back into community ventures.

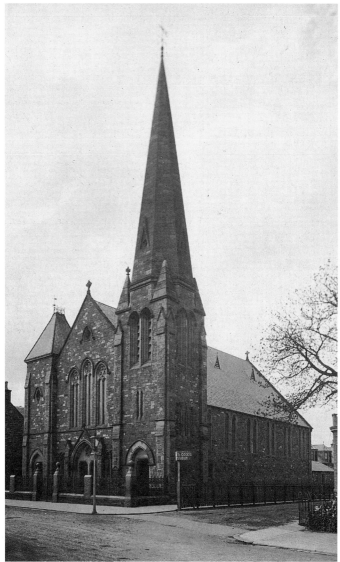

In 1918 the congregations of the West Church and the St Andrews Church were amalgamated and continued to use the West Church building, although it was renamed St Andrews. The old St Andrew's building then became known as the Eastgate Hall and from 1950 was let to the council (who eventually bought it in 1966) for use by youth organisations. Recently, it has been touted as a possible home for the Tweed Theatre Group. A common feature of the entries in the most recent Statistical Account of Scotland, compiled in the 1950s and '60s, was the belief that religious observance by local communities had fallen away since the two world wars. Peebles' Rev. Berry Preston thought that this could be attributed partly to the development of democracy which led people to demand freedom of thought in all areas of life. The two wars (despite being the cause of record attendance figures) also made it common practice to work on a Sunday whereas transport and developments such as the wireless provided alternatives to church going. For all that, Preston felt there was a 'spirit of unselfish service' in the town, there being no shortage of volunteers when charitable organisations needed help.

Despite being established in 1839, Steeples' painting and decorating business was not the oldest of its kind in the town as the Mitchell family's business, acquired from John Turnbull in 1790, was still going strong in the 1930s. In recent years it has continued under the ownership of the Thorburn family. Other decorator firms in the 1930s included Vannan's, Lindsay's, Mason Stevenson's, Hamilton's and J. Mackison & Son.

Young Street is mainly unchanged since this postcard was sent in 1906. The turret on the left-hand side seems to have been a shop at one time and has since been converted into a dwelling.

Formerly known as Acrefield, Rosetta was the name given to the estate lands acquired in the early 1800s by Dr Thomas Young. Young was a retired military surgeon who had done some exploring in his working life, accompanying Sir Ralph Abercromby's expedition to Egypt in 1801. Estate names were often chosen by landowners from amongst their female relatives, but in this case it is likely to be a reference to the Egyptian city where the famous stone which unlocked the secrets of hieroglyphics was discovered in 1799. Rosetta Road has remained a quiet, residential area since this photograph was taken around 1914. Burnett's store at March Street is now a post office.

Kingsland School, off Rosetta Road, was refurbished in the early 1960s and is still in use today. It opened in 1901 to supplement the old Burgh school and its first headmaster was a Mr Todd. At the same time the council also took over Bonnington Academy for use as a high school. Provision of education was always one of Peebles' strengths and a school existed there from as early as 1464. By the late eighteenth century almost 500 pupils were taught at various schools in the town with just over sixty attending its famous Grammar School. Despite this, the poor were still educated at the expense of the church at this time, a situation that would continue for years to come. In his entry for the Second Statistical Account, published in the 1840s, Peebles' minister, Rev. John Elliot, suggested that schoolteachers, 'so useful a class of men', should have their salaries increased according to the rising wealth of the country as a whole, a notion that wouldn't find disagreement with teachers today. By the 1940s Peebles' three schools had been joined by an additional primary building at Halyrude for the Kingsland's infants' Department.

James Kerr set up the *Peebles News and Effectual Advertiser* in 1887. Its premises were initially in Eastgate, moving later to Northgate with a printing works in School Brae. Over its first century the publication had only seven editors, remaining in the Kerr family until 1920 when it was taken over by the Walkers who had launched the *Galashiels Telegraph* in 1896. From this point it became known as the *Peeblesshire News and County Advertiser*. The Kerr connection was still strong, however, as William Kerr became editor after the takeover and stayed in the position for 43 years. In 1963 the newspaper was sold once again, this time to the *Hamilton Advertiser*, although eventually its final home was to be Scottish and Universal Newspapers. The oldest copy of the paper held by the British Newspaper Library dates from 19 December 1896. Back copies dating to the latter years of the nineteenth century, some of them rather the worse for wear, can be viewed at the Advertiser's offices.

FREE TRADE DEMONSTRATION, PEEBLES, Nov. 14th, 1904.

Provost Ballantyne, J.P.
The Master of Ellibank, M.P.   Hon'ble. Mrs. Murray.
Mr. Winston Churchill. M.P.
Sir Thos. Gibson Carmichael.   Lord Dalmeny.

Photo. by McKnaught & Son, Peebles. *What do you think of this.*

The *Peeblesshire Advertiser* and *The Glasgow Herald* reported two very different versions of this demonstration. Ostensibly a meeting to discuss the issue of tax and trade, in practice it became a pre-election tussle between Sir Walter Thorburn MP and the Liberal candidate, the Master of Elibank. Whilst the Peeblesshire paper commented that 'the curtain has fallen upon the greatest political farce which has ever been staged in the county', the *Herald* gave a more sober account. It recorded that the event, held in Peebles' Volunteer Hall, was so well attended that an overflow meeting had to be held at the Chambers Hall. By contrast the Advertiser stated that the extra hall was rented deliberately so as to create the impression that the Liberal candidate was more popular than he actually was. The paper declared that the second meeting had been a 'paper house' and assured the Master of Elibank that he had 'as much chance to reach the North Pole as to head the poll against our present member'. Despite this, he swept the polls in the 1906 election.

33

Mass production of bicycles as we know them today began in the 1890s and prompted the formation of cycle clubs throughout the country. Before then, however various models were tried out with varying degrees of success. Its unlikely that this local lady got far in this impractical looking contraption. Other more ancient pastimes in Peebles included archery, football, horse-racing and play-acting. Archery was practised on the Tweed Green and at Venlaw, but football was less accepted and was banned at the 'Hie Gait' on pain of a substantial fine (eight shillings) and the ball being cut. Throughout the seventeenth century, the Beltane Festival had a horse race as its main event . Records refer to it from 1625 onwards and the winner (the race was between the riders of Nether Horsburgh and East Port) was awarded a bell as a prize. They could keep this until the following year, but by the 1660s the bell was being won outright which was a substantial expense for the competition. Town Council minutes of 1735 state that no horses were entered that year and there was no further mention of the race until the mid-1760s when it was noted that Dr James Hay had ploughed up the common on which it was held.

Canadian Curlers at Peebles Hydro, photographed some time before the First World War. In the past winter curling took place on a pond near the bridge on the south side of the Tweed. Sir John Hay presented Peebles Curling Club with a silver medal in 1823 and this was then played for every year. A further prize was donated in 1830, a massive silver buckle and belt known as 'the Belt of Victory', which was awarded to the winners of an annual competition between the town's married men and the bachelors.

Peebles Golf Club was formed in 1892 and initially played on a rather arduous nine hole course on Morning Hill, about a mile from the town. However, a new eighteen hole course was opened at Kirklands in 1908. The local golfers were very proud of this course and the 'fine' club house. An early tourist attraction, it was strategically positioned within a ten minute walk of the town's two railway stations and visitors were assured that they would be 'heartily welcomed'. During the First World War part of the course was requisitioned by the army and membership fell so much that it was planned to dissolve the club in 1918. The owner of the land, the Earl of Wemyss, agreed to sell and it was bought by the town council who formed a municipal golf course in conjunction with the club. The course had to be redesigned in 1933 when the council decided to use some of its land for housing. After the Second World War, housing shortages led to plans to take almost all of the land for development but luckily for Peebles' golfers and tourists the idea was rejected and the club continues to flourish today.

Peebles' development as a tourist town in the early years of this century relied very much on the sporting amenities it offered and some of the sports clubs around today have long histories. Records of the sixteenth century mention a bowling green on Castle Hill although the club moved to its present site at Walkers Haugh in the mid-1870s. The clubhouse has recently been enlarged and the club itself is still very popular. Peebles Tennis Club is of much later origin, established in 1956, although there was a precursor in the 1930s. In 1970 two of its five courts were upgraded to all weather purposes and a practice wall was also erected that same year. Today, the club averages around 80 members a season.

Formed in 1894, Peebles Rovers played in the East of Scotland League and won the Championship for four years in succession from 1933. In the 1935-36 season the club also reached the final of the Border Cup and the semi-finals of the Scottish Qualifying Cup. J. Dodds had connections with the club of thirty years standing at the time this picture was taken. *Back row (l. to r.):* T. Early, T. Blair, W. Wilson, G. Cochran, W. Rathie, J. Dodds (Trainer). *Front row:* C. McDermont, J. Skedd, G. Waterson (Capt.), J. Gill, J. Kilner, J. Bradley.

The bridge at Manor, the small hamlet near Peebles, was labelled Roman in the nineteenth century with the *laissez-faire* common amongst historians of the time. In fact it was of no older vintage than 1702 and money for its building was paid out of spare church funds for what was considered, 'a most necessary, pious use'. There is an inscription on its side which attributes the building to Lord William Douglas.

Black Dwarf Cottage belonged to David Ritchie, born in Stobo Parish around 1740 and originally known to fellow villagers as 'Bowed Davie' on account of his deformed legs and feet. His later nickname referred to his general mood and outlook on life and a description records that 'his voice was shrill and uncouth, his laugh horrible, and his temper very uncertain'. Unsurprisingly, he sought seclusion and he built his cottage himself in Manor parish. In 1797 Ritchie was visited by Walter Scott and the two got on well supposedly on account of Scott's own disability, a limp. The writer later used Ritchie as the inspiration for the character Elshender the Recluse in his novel *The Black Dwarf*. The original cottage eventually fell into disrepair but local landowner Sir James Nasmyth built another for Ritchie and his sister in 1802. When he died nine years later, Ritchie was buried at Manor churchyard in a grave beside a rowan tree to keep away the witches. His bones were later disinterred and put on display at the Royal College of Surgeons in Edinburgh and his cottage still stands today.

There was shock amongst the Peebles' gentry in 1789 when Kailzie Estate, which dates perhaps from as early as the thirteenth century, was sold to Robert Stoddart. His main income came from his pianoforte factory in London as opposed to inheritance, making him a member of the dreaded *nouveau riche*. He kept the lands for just five years before selling on to Robert Nutter Campbell who made improvements to the house which was then left unmodified for the next seventy years. Many country residences such as Kailzie were seen off during the twentieth century for a variety of reasons. Some were requisitioned as hospitals or barracks during the two world wars or were abandoned because of a crisis in the family finances. Others were lucky enough to be reinvented such as Calderpark Estate in Lanarkshire which was developed into a zoo. Although Kailzie estate was preserved as public gardens (still one of Peebles' attractions today) its mansion house was demolished in 1957.

Whim House apparently got its name from its conception as 'a fit of caprice by a nobleman'. The land's original name, Blair Bog, describes perfectly its pre-developed state as a virtual quagmire, constantly waterlogged with no shelter. In 1730 it was bought by the Earl of Islay who, primarily for his own amusement, started a lengthy battle to tame it. A house was built first and then a drainage system was installed, drawing off water to create a small lake elsewhere. These drains were constantly failing because their moss walls crumbled easily and had to be repeatedly rebuilt. The Earl died in 1763 and the estate was bought a couple of years later by James Montgomery (who was instrumental in abolishing serfdom in Scotland). Legend has it that he found wine in the cellars equal in value to what he had paid for the property. Montgomery continued the Earl's improvements including extensions to the house and today it still stands and is in use as an old folk's home.

W.R.&S. 22606. GIPSY GLEN, PEEBLES.

The old Drove Road passed through Peebles via the Gipsy Glen. Because they were used mainly for transporting sheep and cattle, roads such as this were exempt from the tolls charged on parish and turnpike roads and livestock taken through Peebles were also allowed to rest on what was known as the King's Muir (later the site of the Caledonian station) for a small fee. Today Gipsy Glen is undeveloped and still known by this name although no gipsies have camped here in living memory. What stories there are date from centuries ago, such as the deadly fracas between two gipsy families, the Faws and the Shaws, in 1677. On returning from the Haddington Fair the families got into a fight which left Sandie Faw and his pregnant wife dead. Robin Shaw and his three sons were hanged for this the following year at the Grassmarket. A Dr Pennicuik commemorated the incident by erecting a dove-cot inscribed with the rather morbid inscription, 'The field of Gipsie blood which here you see / A shelter to the harmless dove shall be.'

12 ON SOONHOPE BURN, PEEBLES

Soonhope Farm (originally Swynhope) belonged to the Smithfield family before it was bought by Dr Hay of Haystoun. About a quarter of a mile from Peebles on the road to Innerleithen, Soonhope Valley was once scattered with Celtic forts and at its north end are the remains of a medieval castle. From at least 1864 Peebles got its water supply from this district. During the twentieth century the area was developed as a holiday camp and its chalets are still popular with Edinburgh visitors.

The cottage at Whitebrig, about one and a half miles outside Peebles, was the premises of the Bruce family's smiddy. It was abandoned some time in the 1950s but has since been refurbished for use as a residence.

Stobo probably owes its existence chiefly to the Norman church which dates from 1127, although a part of it (known as the Cell of St Kentigern and restored in 1929) goes as far back as the sixth century. This building functions as a historical record of Stobo's past: marks on the stone porch date from the twelfth century and were made by men sharpening arrow-heads; the church holds the tomb of a fifteenth century dignitary; and the building is decorated with sixteenth century Italian lamps. The first record of the name of the parish dates from the 1100s and appears as 'Stoboc', while variations such as Stobhope and Stobhowe have led some to believe the name means 'the hollow of stumps' (perhaps as a result of an ancient forest fire). Whatever the origins of its name, the parish has long been famed for its rural prettiness, moving one writer in the 1950s to florid heights of description: 'Its hills . . . glow with fine trees the colour of the purple heather in August and from whose bosom tumbling burns offer their tribute to the young Tweed'.

Chiefly agricultural throughout its past, Stobo's position near the Tweed meant that its lands were particularly suited for pasture and this gave its butter and milk a superior flavour. By 1950 there were still nine working farms. Most of these made a living rearing stock, although two were combined dairy and sheep concerns. Elsewhere, agriculture was in decline. Rev. Auld, writer of the Third Statistical Account, was concerned that the large estates were becoming run down, attributing blame to the socialist government of the day. 'The high cost of labour makes proper maintenance inside and outside the houses of all but the working class a serious burden.' One of the few alternative industries in Stobo's past were its slate quarries which produced dark blue slate used to roof many of its ancient buildings but no coal was ever discovered in the parish and it had to be imported either from mines in the Lothians, or from Douglas Coal Hill or Wilsontown.

Stobo's educational facilities reflected its small population which in the 1790s was estimated to be just 318. Throughout the eighteenth and nineteenth centuries one school was sufficient. In 1790 this had just 24 pupils paying a shilling a quarter to learn to read (writing and arithmetic cost an extra sixpence). In the early 1830s, to encourage attendance, Sir James Montgomery of Stobo Castle paid the school fees of any family which sent more than two children. (The Montgomeries were well-known as zealous improvers, Sir James' father being the first to grow turnips and to use the two-horse plough in Peeblesshire!) By 1950 children over the age of twelve travelled to school in Peebles, a policy some believed contributed to the deterioration of community life around this period. Many parishioners travelled to work in Peebles at the tweedmills and found their entertainments outwith Stobo and this inevitably led to a decline in its own facilities. In 1950 Stobo ceased to be a separate parish (merging with Drumelzier) and had its railway station closed down in the same year.